Sonnets of David 3:
Books IV - V

Sonnets of David

Sonnets of David 3:
Books IV-V

A Poetic Paraphrase of Psalms 90-150

Robert Hellam

iUniverse, Inc.
New York Lincoln Shanghai

Sonnets of David 3: Books IV-V
A Poetic Paraphrase of Psalms 90-150

iUniverse, Inc.

For information address:
iUniverse
2021 Pine Lake Road, Suite 100
Lincoln, NE 68512
www.iuniverse.com

ISBN: 0-595-28412-4 (Pbk)
ISBN: 0-595-65788-5 (Cloth)

Printed in the United States of America

To the Muse, the Counselor, the Comforter Who comes alongside

"This shall be written for the generation to come: and the people which shall be created shall praise the LORD."

—*Psalm 102:18*

Contents

Foreword

These poems were written between November 2001 and June 2003. Perhaps this third volume took longer to write than the second volume because of the author's choice to approximate the acrostic features of Psalms 111, 112, 119, and 145. It would be tempting to go back and rewrite the paraphrases of Psalms 25, 34, and 37 in a similar manner—but there is something of a feel of finality to a piece of writing once it has been published, so maybe it is better to leave those earlier poems as they are. Though the actual writing of the poems in these three volumes took about five and a half years, the time between the composition of the first one in 1986 and the last one in 2003 has been almost a third of the writer's lifetime!

Preface

Some Bible versions divide the book of Psalms into five "books," the fourth of them containing Psalms 90-106 and the fifth Psalms 107-150; hence the title of this book: *Sonnets of David 3: Books IV-V.*

Acknowledgments

I am grateful to the faculty, staff, and student body at Monterey Bay Christian School for providing me the opportunity to work at a job that I truly love, where I can serve God and His people. May He richly bless the Class of 2003, who, as I write this, just graduated yesterday; and our principal, Cheryl Hinton, and elementary-school vice principal, Christel Reed—who, at this writing, are about to go on to other endeavors.

Thanks also to Seaside Assembly of God, our school's sponsoring church; and to First Baptist Church of Seaside, the host church of our middle-school campus.

I would also like to acknowledge my own teachers at Del Rey Woods Elementary School, Fremont Junior High School, and Monterey High School—particularly, my second-grade teacher, the late Vivian Kernohan; my eighth-grade English teacher, the late Charles Crary; and my high-school English teachers, Richard Lundy, Frank Jacobson, and the late David Maat.

My mother-in-law of blessed memory, Encarnacion Cristobal, was as proud of me as if I had been her own son. She kept a clipping of everything that I ever wrote for publication. May she be allowed a peek down this way, from where she resides in the presence of God, to share some satisfaction at the completion of this project.

And, as always, I especially thank my dear wife (and fellow teacher at Monterey Bay Christian School), Connie Hellam, for all her help, encouragement, and constructive criticism.

Introduction

This may be the first time that all the Psalms have been paraphrased into English-language sonnets. (If this is not true, I hope that someone more knowledgeable than I will correct me.) Certainly, every psalm has been made into a *poem* of some kind in English, but as far as I know no author has before rendered every single one into a *sonnet* in our language. The Spanish author Francisco de Quevedo, a contemporary of Cervantes and Shakespeare, paraphrased at least some of the Psalms into sonnets, but I have not discovered whether he did so with the whole Psalter. Even if he did, I believe that this present work may be a first in our own tongue.

In reviewing the introductory material in the previous volumes, I find that I have failed to acknowledge adequately some of those who have helped me and influenced me in my career as a poet. My mother, Phyllis Hellam, played an essential role when she taught me to read, after my first-grade teacher (whom I remember as a very kind and conscientious lady) had apparently concluded that I was just not going to reach that goal in the classroom. My mother is herself an award-winning writer of poetry and fiction. And then there have been several other poets whom I might call "poetry partners."

My college roommate, Bill Scott, was a great encouragement as another writer of prose and poetry and as my first publisher. Bill was editor of *The Roc*, a literary magazine that he founded at Cowell College, at the University of California at Santa Cruz (where I was a student for two years, before dropping out to join the Navy), in about 1965. During that same time period, Joe Cristobal, a childhood friend who would later become my brother-in-law, was also very important. In the late 1960's, Joe and I used to share our poems with each other on an almost-daily basis.

And I should not fail to mention, as an influence on me, a book that was given to me by Joe Cristobal. In 1986, just before I began this project, Vikram Seth's *The Golden Gate* appeared. This is a novel set in San Francisco in the 1980's, written entirely in sonnet-like stanzas. (Another of my poet friends has criticized the book for portraying sexually immoral characters, but in the author's defense it must be pointed out that he was merely trying to show San Francisco as he saw it.) The book was, in my opinion, a masterpiece, and it demonstrated that perhaps there was a market in our time for an entire volume of poetry on a connected theme. (For a recent example of a sonnet on an explicitly Biblical subject, see "Professor Carver's Bible Class," in Marilyn Nelson's excellent biography in verse of George Washington Carver.)

C. F. Stevens ("Steve") was my fellow toiler in the Federal bureaucracy for many years. He and I shared our literary works with each other, and his dry wit helped to make government work bearable. Steve's poems were a worthy tribute to his master, Kipling, and he was the one who introduced me to the sestina, a rather difficult form that Kipling had handled well. With his typical humorous flair, Steve even developed a "sestina worksheet," a pattern for the would-be writer, in a style similar to that of the numerous worksheets used in a Social Security office for various routine and tedious calculations.

My friend and mentor Rev. Dr. Dean Koontz, who has himself paraphrased some psalms into rhyming poetry, was kind enough to read and comment on the poems in my first volume, after the poems and introduction had been written but before they were published. And, also after the writing but before the publication of my first volume, the late Mary Wilson read and commented on all the poems therein, painstakingly analyzing their phonetic patterns. Her self-published collection of poetry was an inspiration to me, showing me that one could indeed put forth one's poems to the public without going begging from one major publisher to another.

Van Vradenburg, the vice principal at the middle-school campus where I teach, has also been a poetry partner and a great encourager. He and I have shared our writings with each other for the last several years and spurred each other on to accomplishing our poetic goals. Both my sons have written rather good poetry, and Brian, our younger son, helped me to improve what I had thought was my final draft of Psalm 130, his favorite psalm.

Last Christmas I received from two of my students, the Couch sisters, a gift that has really blessed me: a collection of Amy Carmichael's poems. Miss Carmichael has perhaps captured the essence of the Psalms in the last five words of her meditation on Psalm 97:11, when she sings, "Lord, Thy love we praise!"

If these three volumes of poetry that I have now completed have blessed you, Reader, then please remember that no writer really works alone. And, of course, far beyond any human help, God is the main Actor in all our lives and deserves credit and honor and glory as the Author of all good things.—*Seaside, California, June 5, 2003*

Note on the Bibliography: The same sources were consulted as for the first two volumes. Also looked at were the additional resources listed in the Bibliography of the present volume.

Book IV
Psalms 90-106

Psalm 90
Prayer of Moses the Man of God

Lord, our existence always was in You
Before we lived, before the world began.
Are mountains small to You—millennia, too?
Then in Your eyes what is this thing called man?
From dust we came. To dust we must return.
Our lives fly like the hour before the dawn.
As grass springs up just for the sun to burn,
We wither up, dry out, and soon are gone.
For nothing stands against Your searching gaze—
No sin of ours is hidden from Your sight.
In fear and pain we pass away our days.
Your wrath oppresses us, but You are right!
Deserving nothing but Your condemnation,
We live in vain and die in sheer frustration.

Though we might survive for seventy years,
Or even eighty, maybe—it could be—
Yet life would still be hard and full of tears,
Our days still fade away as fleetingly.
No one can estimate Your anger's might.
Your worth no one can fully recognize.
Teach us to value life, to judge it right,
That we might have a heart both just and wise.
How long, Lord, till You fill us full of bliss,
Till we awake and sing ecstatically
As that day's joy outweighs the woe of this,
Your mighty works the only thing we see?
Though nothing that we do in this life stands,
Our God, please bless the labor of our hands.

Psalm 91
The Shadow of the Almighty

Whoever lives within God's lofty hall
Will always be protected in its shade.
I say, "The Lord is like a castle wall,
My Refuge, God. My trust He has repaid."
And like a mother bird with young offspring,
My God will keep you from the fowler's snare,
Will cover you beneath His mighty wing.
From every danger you find safety there.
Though arrows fly by day, and fears by night,
Diseases prowl the dark and plague the noon,
A thousand die—ten thousand—on your right,
Our faithful God will save His children soon.
But you will see, with your own eyes observe,
The wicked get the doom that they deserve.

If you, as well, will in the Lord abide,
Seek refuge, as I do, in God Most High,
No harm can touch you, resting safe inside.
Disasters pass your dwellingplace right by.
For He will send His angels, as He said,
Upholding you lest you should stub your toe.
Upon the deadly adder you will tread,
And trample lions underfoot, also.
"The one who loves Me I will save from all,
Defend the one who knows My holy Name
And answer him whenever he may call,
That he may have protection and acclaim.
To satisfy him, long life I bestow,
To him who loves Me, My salvation show."

Psalm 92
An Ode for the Sabbath Day

It's good to praise You, Lord, both day and night
And make sweet music to Your Name Most High,
To sing Your faithful love by morning's light,
Proclaim it still when sunset stains the sky.
We pluck a melody from rows of strings
To celebrate Your works, Your every action.
Excited, glad, my voice rejoicing sings,
Expressing my delight, my satisfaction.
Your works are vast, my Lord, Your thoughts profound,
Magnificent the products of Your hand.
But evil men and evil deeds abound,
And foolish ones will never understand—
The wicked thrive, but soon their time is past.
They die like weeds. Your glory, Lord, will last.

Your enemies, my Lord, will disappear,
Will perish from the earth in deep disgrace
Or run away from You in utter fear,
Afraid to stand before Your wrathful face.
But me You strengthen like a bison's horn,
Anointing me with oil so clear and fine.
And, pampered like a precious unicorn,
I know that I am Yours and You are mine.
Now You have let me see my enemies
Destroyed, defeated. Yes, their time was short!
Your righteous ones will thrive like mighty trees,
Like palm trees planted in the Temple court.
And when they're old, still green, their fruitfulness
Will still declare the Lord's great righteousness.

Psalm 93
A Rising Tide of Praise

The Lord God reigns, attired in majesty,
Yes, clothed with majesty and armed with might.
This world He made is built so sturdily
It will not topple, founded firm and tight.
God's throne, beyond that, stands eternally.
Great seas, our Lord, have raised their waters high,
Have raised their mighty voice. The roaring sea
Has raised up crashing waves. Their waters fly
Before the power of the Lord of all,
For You are stronger than the howling ocean
And stronger than the high tide's moving wall.
And strong, Lord, is Your people's firm devotion.
Eternally unchanging is Your Word,
And beautiful Your holy Temple, Lord.

Psalm 94
Just Deserts

Avenging God, our Lord, in vengeance blaze
Against the proud and wicked of the earth
And make them understand that God repays.
How long, my Lord, must we endure their mirth?
They spew out arrogance. They always boast
As they assault Your loved ones, Lord, with glee.
The most forlorn and weak they hurt the most
And say, "God takes no notice, does not see."
Get wise, you fools! God made the eye, the ear.
God made the Law. His judgment is not slow.
How can you dream that He won't see or hear?
You think the Source of knowledge will not *know*?
Men's empty thoughts look good in human eyes—
But only God, Who knows all thoughts, is wise.

How happy he, the one whom You chastise,
Who learns Your Law, while sinners earn their fate.
Us chosen ones You never will despise,
Your followers, the heirs of Your estate.
Against the wicked who will side with me?
Without You, Lord, I surely would have died,
For when my foot slid out so suddenly,
You held me up. My soul is satisfied.
Do evil rulers reign "by right divine"?
They put the righteous head upon the block.
Against Your Law their counselors combine.
But You, my Lord, my Fortress, are my Rock.
My God will right all wrong one certain day,
All sinful pride will certainly repay.

Psalm 95
Unto Him with Psalms

Come praise the Lord with joy. Now let us sing!
With gratitude we lift Him up in song.
To Him, Rock of Salvation, mighty King,
We shout with strength, for He alone is strong.
For high above, above all "gods," is He
Whose hand holds deepest depths and mountains high
And formed the dry land and surrounding sea,
Who made us, all who dwell below the sky.
So worship Him, then. Bow and bend your knee
To God our Lord, Whose humble sheep we are.
"Now hear My voice," God says. "Attend to Me,
Unlike your ancestors, who wandered far.
For forty years, they put Me to the test.
I vowed in wrath, 'They shall not know My rest.'"

Psalm 96
The Ark of the Covenant

Oh, sing the Lord a new song, all the earth,
Yes, sing to Him and praise His holy Name.
Proclaim salvation. Sing His matchless worth
Among the heathen. God's great works acclaim!
For He is great, above all "gods." Now praise
The One Who made the heavens, all you lands,
And give to Him His glory all your days,
And give to Him the treasure in your hands.
In trembling fear adore the one true Lord
Who firmly reigns and will return one day.
Let heaven, earth, and sea in one great chord
Ring out in joy! Why, even trees will pray,
Will sing before the Lord, Who will return
To judge all men. His justice they will learn.

Psalm 97
Let the Earth Rejoice

Our good Lord reigns. Rejoice in all the world.
Let distant isles take joy in Him alone.
Around Him clouds of dark are thickly furled,
And righteousness upholds His holy throne.
His foes will burn in fire, His lightnings shake
Created things, as mountains melt away,
God's glory evident. Make no mistake—
Idolaters, give up your dolls of clay!
God's righteousness makes Zion ring with joy
And Judah's many villages rejoice.
He guards His own from those who would destroy.
Our Lord Most High, please hear our gladsome voice:
God's light and joy bless people freed from blame.
Rejoice, you righteous. Praise His holy Name!

Psalm 98
A New Song

Now sing a new song. Praise our mighty Lord!
To all, He has announced His great salvation,
Victorious His right hand and mighty sword.
His righteousness is plain to every nation—
They see His steadfast love for Israel.
In joyful worship all Creation sings—
His glorious deeds we all remember well!
Musicians, sound the brass and strum the strings.
Israel, Gentiles, each created thing,
Together make majestic harmony
In joyful homage to the Lord, the King,
Above the rhythmic rumble of the sea.
Let rivers clap and mountains sing in chorus
When God the Judge comes down with justice for us.

Psalm 99
The Lord Reigns

In Zion reigns the Lord—the nations shake—
Between the cherubim He sits in state,
So let the very earth in terror quake,
For He is high, above all nations, great.
Yes, He is holy. Praise His wondrous Name!
All righteousness derives from this great King.
To Jacob, He in love and justice came.
So worship. Lift Him high in everything.
Yes, He is holy. Moses knew Him well.
When Aaron, Samuel, called upon His Name,
God did forgive His people, Israel,
Though He chastised them when they were to blame.
And at His holy hill, lift up, applaud,
And worship. Holy is the Lord our God.

Psalm 100
Make a Joyful Noise

All earth, now burst with joy, and gladly shout!
Yes, make a thankful clamor to the Lord.
Exultantly exalt Him. Sing right out
To let Him hear that He is most adored.
Now worship Him, for God alone is He
Who made us, since we are not self-created
And we are not our own. His sheep are we.
For us, His greatness has He demonstrated.
So enter through His gates with great thanksgiving
And let His Temple's courts resound with praise.
Without Him, there would be no people living.
Then bless His Name, today and all your days!
Forever—from now on, as in the past—
Our Lord is good. His steadfast love will last.

Psalm 101
King David's Song

Of You, Your love, Your justice, Lord, I sing
And praise You as I walk with blameless heart,
My eyes ignoring every evil thing
And yearning for You. Must we be apart?
To unbelievers, Lord, I will not cling—
They are the sort I do not want to know.
No room for them have I, a godly king.
All slanderers, all liars, have to go.
My eyes seek out the faithful everywhere
For blameless servants who will dwell with me.
I will reject all those who falsely swear,
And cast out those who speak untruthfully.
Yes, I will purge the wicked from Your land,
Your holy city, Lord. They must not stand.

Psalm 102
A Prayer of the Afflicted

Please hear my prayer, my Lord, my cry for aid,
And do not turn from me, saddest of souls.
Please listen, for my life begins to fade,
My days like smoke, my bones like burning coals.
My heart, a wilted weed, is desiccated.
I groan, forget to eat, all bones and skin,
A lonely owl or buzzard, isolated,
A little lonesome sparrow, weak and thin.
All day, my foes their fulsome taunts rehearse.
I dine on ashes, my own tears for drink.
My name, dishonored, has become a curse.
In wrath You cast me out. My spirits sink.
My life's at twilight. It will soon be done.
I fade away like weeds in summer's sun.

Lord, You, however, never fade away.
All generations look to You in trust.
Please favor Zion now. This is her day.
Your servants love her very stones and dust!
All nations, Lord, will speak Your Name in fear.
Their kings will see Your glory fill their eyes.
In Zion, built again, You will appear
In answer to Your people's pleading cries.
For future generations be it stated
And written down to God Almighty's praise
That He looked down, the captives liberated,
And kept grim death from shortening their days.
In Zion, praise the Lord. His Name declare.
All kings, all nations, come to worship there.

As I began to age, my strength grew weak.
It seemed my days were nearly at an end.
Distressed, to God I then began to speak:
"You surely have more time that You could lend,
For You made time, earth, heaven, with Your hand.
They all will perish. You live past all days.
When all is fallen, only You will stand.
All else will wear out, as old clothing frays.
But in the end You will renew all things.
You, always young, forever old, will stand.
Of You, eternal God, this anthem sings—
Of You, Who hold Your people in Your hand.
Descendants of Your servants, Lord, will live,
A guarantee that You alone can give."

Psalm 103
Bless the Lord, O My Soul

Praise the Lord, my soul. Bless His holy Name.
Praise the Lord, my soul. Forget not His deeds,
Who heals, forgives you, saves from death and blame,
Renews you like an eagle, fills your needs.
Restoring justice, working righteousness,
Our Lord let Moses know His ways full well,
Redeeming those whom Pharaoh did oppress,
Displaying miracles to Israel.
Choosing to love, His anger in reserve,
Our Lord is not accusing us of wrong
Or dealing with our sins as they deserve.
His strong compassion has persisted long,
His love for us high as the heavens are,
Our sins like east from west—removed that far!

A father, for his children, has compassion.
So does the Lord, for people who revere Him.
He knows us—little ones whom He did fashion—
And in His mercy, He allows us near Him.
A man lasts hardly longer than a weed,
A flower of the field that blows away,
Its very memory erased with speed.
From *"Let there be…"* till after the last day,
The Lord is near to people who revere Him,
Who listen to His Law and know His way.
In kingly power, there is no one near Him.
Praise the Lord, you angels. Praise and obey.
Praise the Lord, all things under His control.
All creation, praise! Praise the Lord, my soul.

Psalm 104
How Manifold Are Thy Works!

Praise the Lord, my soul. God, You are so great,
Enrobed in glory, light, and majesty
Behind the skies that curtain Your estate,
Its pillars firmly fixed upon the sea.
Clouds are Your carriage, Your pathway the air.
You made Your angels just by breathing out—
They move like flames, from You to everywhere.
You laid the earth's foundations, strong and stout.
Though earth once lay beneath the mighty sea,
That flood diminished, fled before Your face,
And—shrinking from the mountains suddenly—
Poured down the valleys to its proper place.
The seas obey Your will, for they are bound
And nevermore will inundate the ground.

God sends the waters down the mountain passes
To carry life. He pours them from above
To satisfy the cattle and the asses.
Well-watered trees bear birds who sing for love.
He waters all His mountains from on high.
A grateful earth responds in fruitfulness.
He grows the grass, makes farm crops multiply,
Gives wine and oil and bread, our hearts to bless.
Yes, watered well, God's forests touch the sky,
His cedars tall in Lebanon up north
Fine homes for birds, the storks' nests far up high.
From pine to pine, small birds slip back and forth.
The mountain goat across the summit strides,
While in the rocks the bashful badger hides.

Your moon marks time. Your sun knows when to set.
You made the dark, when lions prowl by night
And roar for meat. From You their food they get.
At sunrise, they slink home in stealthy flight.
Then man goes out to labor all the day.
In wisdom You have made this vast creation.
Your oceans teem with life. The great whales play,
While ships ply to and fro for every nation.
All look to You for food at times awaited
And gladly take things from Your open hand,
As with delight their appetites are sated.
When You seem far away, they cannot stand.
When You withhold the breath from men, they die.
You send Your Spirit, new life to supply.

Then may His glory last beyond all time,
Beyond forever, past all years, all days,
And may He view His handiwork sublime,
And may our Lord take joy from it, and praise.
Now if the Lord but looks upon the earth,
This vast creation shakes upon its frame.
Those mountains seem to be quite stout of girth,
But should He touch them, they would smoke and flame.
So I will sing to God for all my days,
Exalting Him as long as I shall live,
My songs exploding forth in bursts of praise,
Sweet meditations such as I can give.
Let this please God, Whom gladly I extol,
And may evil cease. Praise the Lord, my soul.

Psalm 105
Sing Psalms

Praise the Lord. Give thanks. Call upon His Name.
Rejoice, and tell the world, and sing His praise.
Proclaim His glory, seek Him, spread His fame,
Receive His strength. Yes, seek Him all your days.
Children of Abraham, remember ever,
Our Lord remembers always His command
To give to you, the sons and heirs, forever,
Of Abraham, Isaac, Jacob, the land.
His chosen ones were small in population
And wandered through the country like a stranger
From place to place, outsiders in each nation,
But God let no one put them into danger.
God warned the foreign kings He had appointed,
"Harm not My people. Touch not My anointed."

God sent a famine on the Promised Land
And sent a man ahead, a lowly slave,
Imprisoned, chained and shackled foot and hand,
Who would the future tell, the kingdom save.
Then sent the king to set this poor man free,
Exalting him in everybody's eyes,
Set him to rule the kingdom faithfully,
Imparting godly wisdom to the wise.
So Israel came to stay in Egypt land,
To live as strangers in a foreign nation.
Then God made Egypt close their open hand
And made them fear this growing population.
He hardened them to act in enmity,
To treat His people underhandedly.

His servants—Moses, Aaron—did He send
To work His wonders over Egypt land,
Which proudly did against His word offend.
Thick darkness covered all, at His command.
All waters turned to blood. The fish all died.
Loud frogs invaded palaces of kings.
God spoke. Then came the bugs, outside, inside,
Annoying insects swarming on all things.
Instead of rain, great hailstones crashed the ground,
Destroying vines and figs and every tree.
God spoke. Then locust armies came around
To eat up every plant that they could see.
On man and beast He caused dark death to fall—
He killed the firstborn males among them all.

Our Lord brought Israel out of slavery,
Ensuring that their wealth was multiplied.
Egyptians let them go out willingly
Because they dreaded God, His people's Guide.
His people asked for food. He brought them meat.
With heaven's bread He did their bodies bless.
He opened rocks, and out gushed water sweet
That flowed like rivers in the wilderness.
For God the Lord had made a sacred vow.
Remembering His servant Abraham,
He brought His people from their exile now,
With joyful shout, from out the land of Ham.
They took the heathens' lands, their golden hoard,
To be God's faithful people. Praise the Lord.

Psalm 106
All the People Say, "Amen"

Praise the Lord. Give Him thanks, for He is good.
But who can tell His mighty deeds, His love,
And who can praise Him fully as we should?
Happy the righteous, guided from above.
Remember me, Lord, when You save the nation,
So I may join in praising gratefully.
We sin, as did our fathers' generation,
When they were filled with doubt beside the sea.
Yet You were faithful. Just when hope had fled,
You saved them all from mighty Pharaoh's hand.
Your people crossed the waters' dried-up bed—
Not one Egyptian lived to reach the land.
When crashing waters drowned the Hebrews' foes,
Then they believed in God. Their praise arose.

But they forgot the deeds that God had done
And would not wait to hear what He would say.
They tested Him beneath the desert sun.
He slaked their thirst, but sent disease their way.
Resenting Moses, rebels stirred them up
To envy leaders God had consecrated.
Abiram, Dathan—He interred them. Up
Came fire on them, and they were immolated.
And then God's people made a golden bull
To worship in the place of God's great glory,
Forgetting God, Whose wrath was at the full
At those who lived out, yet forgot, His story.
God would have crushed them with His mighty reach,
If not for Moses standing in the breach.

They would not even take the Promised Land—
In their great unbelief, the people grumbled.
Their Lord then promised them, by His own hand,
That they would die. Their offspring would be humbled.
They joined themselves with heathen enemies,
Uniting in blasphemy with Moabites
And honoring their lifeless effigies
By eating offerings from pagan rites.
Their wickedness brought down the wrath of God,
Who sent a plague where many thousands died
Till Phinehas boldly acted, stayed God's rod,
And earned his fame. But by the waters' side,
Irate on God's behalf, rash Moses spoke
At Meribah, God's anger to provoke.

God's people would not slay their enemies
But stayed among them, copying their ways
And worshiping their evil effigies,
For whom they gave their children to the blaze.
By offering their offspring to the devil,
Smirching themselves, staining the land with blood,
They brought themselves down to the heathens' level.
Our Lord's great wrath came on them like a flood.
He put them under rule of foreign nations.
Each time He saved them, they became transgressors.
At last, the cry of many generations
Made God put mercy into their oppressors.
Lord, save us. Bring us home, that we may raise
Thanksgiving to Your Name, triumphal praise.

Praise to the Lord, the God of Israel.
Yes, praise Him now, and evermore as well.
Let all the gathered people say, "Amen!"
Then praise the Lord, and praise the Lord again.

Book V
Psalms 107-150

Psalm 107
The Redeemed of the Lord

Give thanks. The Lord is good, His love forever.
So will His rescued people now declare,
Those gathered from all places whatsoever,
From north, south, east, and west, from everywhere.
Some, starving, found no refuge anywhere
But wandered through the thirsty wilderness.
They cried out to the Lord in their despair,
And He delivered them from all distress.
He led them straight to their new dwellingplace,
A city made to give them satisfaction.
So, people, thank Him for His mighty grace,
For all He does for you, His every action.
For thirsty throats, He sends forth soothing springs,
And fills the hungry up with all good things.

Some rebels, chained in darkness, suffered there
Because they had despised God's righteousness.
They cried out to the Lord in their despair,
And He delivered them from all distress.
He brought them from that dark and gloomy place—
Bronze gates, strong bars, for Him are no distraction.
So, people, thank Him for His mighty grace,
For all He does for you, His every action.
Some foolish ones were facing death's cold stare.
They cried out to the Lord from that hard place,
And He delivered them from dark despair.
So, people, thank Him for His mighty grace,
For all He does for you, His every action.
Then praise! Give thanks, in joyful satisfaction.

When merchants went in ships upon the seas,
A mighty storm stirred them to stupefaction.
In fear and awe, they fell upon their knees.
They saw the Lord's stupendous strength in action.
They pitched and rolled, in fear and shock did stare,
Staggered as in a state of drunkenness.
They cried out to the Lord in their despair,
And He delivered them from all distress.
He stilled the storm (and calmness took its place),
Led them to port, to their great satisfaction.
So, people, thank Him for His mighty grace,
For all He does for you, His every action.
Exalt Him, people, in the congregation,
And praise Him, seasoned elders of the nation.

Then God turned rivers into wilderness
And fruitful fields into a barren ground,
For those who dwelt there lived in wickedness.
But for His own, He turned it all around—
He dotted desert land with pleasant pools,
Watered the thirsty ground with flowing springs.
He made the earth respond to farming tools
And filled the hungry with delightful things.
Their children, crops, and livestock kept increasing,
Until disaster came on them again.
But God reversed the course of their decreasing.
Rejoice, you saints! Hush up, you wicked men.
You who are wise, consider carefully
The Lord's enormous love for you and me.

Psalm 108
Victory for the Anointed

My heart awakes to sing and give You praise,
To give You glory with the sound of strings
Before all people, everywhere, always.
Your truth and mercy oversee all things.
Exult, my soul. Exalt your Lord. Bow down.
Lord, with Your hand, Your dear ones please deliver.
Judah is Your scepter, Ephraim Your crown,
As You rule east and west banks of the river.
"In Moab," says our God, "I wash My feet,
And toss My sandal where I will in Edom.
Philistia, My triumph is complete!"
Oh, God, You took us back and won our freedom.
No human help could beat our enemy.
By God alone we have the victory!

Psalm 109
Yea, I Will Praise Him

Oh, God, I call on You, the One I praise,
To speak on my behalf. Please don't keep mum,
For I have undergone some trying days.
Deceitful, lying words against me come
From men whose hateful tongues say nothing true,
Whose mouths, like savage beasts', are open wide,
Attacking me. My God, I call on You.
Surrounded now, I need a place to hide.
I gave no cause for their attacks on me—
Despite them, I have tried to be their friend,
Yet they keep on accusing viciously,
And I will keep on praying to the end.
They pay me bad for good, sad to relate,
And for my friendly acts they show me hate.

Subject my foe to evil machinations,
Accusers on his right hand, in his face.
May his sad pleas bring only condemnations.
Cut short his life. Let someone take his place.
His high position gone, his wife alone,
His children wander homeless, fatherless.
His goods will go to satisfy a loan,
As strangers feed upon his thriftiness.
May no one show him kindness, none at all,
His bad repute stain his posterity,
And may the Lord his forebears' sins recall
(His mother's name a shameful memory),
Repay his parents' deeds, who gave him birth,
Erase their reputations from the earth.

For he would never think of showing kindness,
But victimized the needy and the poor,
Would curse, not bless. Repay his spirit's blindness—
Yes, let his curses rest at his own door.
Since curses were the clothes he loved to wear,
May they be wrapped around him good and tight,
Forever squeezing, choking out the air.
Lord, thus repay my foes. It serves them right!
But treat me well, Lord. Glorify Your Name.
Deliver me, because of Your great love,
For I am needy, poor, cast down by shame,
A shadow gone as night falls from above.
Weak-kneed and splinter-thin, I feel forlorn,
As my accusers look on me with scorn.

My Lord, my God, I call to You for aid,
For You will save me, out of Your great love,
And all will know the difference You have made
In reaching down Your hand from up above.
They curse me. You will bless. I know You will,
As my attackers flee confusedly
And I rejoice. I will be joyful still
When they are clothed in shame from neck to knee.
My mouth will open, shouting out God's praise,
Exalting Him among the congregation.
To glorify Him, glad cries will I raise,
Exclaiming ringing words of celebration.
Against this poor man's foes, at my right hand,
To save from base attacks, the Lord will stand.

Psalm 110
Priest and King

To my Lord says the Lord, "To My right hand
Now come, be honored, take the favored seat.
From Zion You will rule in every land,
Your enemies a footstool for Your feet."
Your willing troops majestically arrayed,
Your holy beauty glistens like the dew.
God's vow is not denied and not delayed:
"Melchizedek was priest. Like him are You,
Eternal Priest." With God at Your right hand,
All nations You will judge, give life or death,
Hold power over kings of every land,
Who fear Your wrath and heed Your every breath.
From brooks beside the way, the Lord gives drink
To my Lord, lifts His head above the brink.

Psalm 111
The ABC's of Worship

Alleluia! The Lord be ever praised.
Before the congregation I will speak,
Commending Him. For Him my voice is raised.
Delight in all His works, and be amazed!
Exceeding all our thoughts, He is unique,
For all who ponder Him are dazzled, dazed.
Great are His mighty deeds. You must not seek
His thoughts to understand. He is the peak
In majesty and righteousness forever.
Just look at all His works. Think not to find
Knowledge beyond His revelation. Never
Lose sight of His compassion. He is kind,
Merciful giver to those who revere Him,
Minding His promise to keep us all near Him.

Now for His people He has shown His might.
Of other nations they will have the rule.
Permitted by the Lord, they have that right.
Quite faithful is the Lord, and as a jewel
Reflects bright light, so does His righteousness
Shine in the clarity of His commands
That stand forever and will always bless.
Upright and true are all things from His hands.
Very faithful is He, holy, sublime.
When He redeemed His people from their fetters,
X marked the spot where He signed for all time
Yahweh, His Name, too pure for human letters.
Zealous to fear our great Lord you must be,
Zestful to praise Him, His wisdom to see.

Psalm 112
Alpha and Omega

Alleluia! Now give the Lord applause.
Blessed is the person who will fear Him,
Choosing to take delight in all His laws.
Down the generations God is near him,
Ever to bless his children day and night,
For his descendants will know happiness.
Goods uncountable fill his house by right,
His offspring ever knowing blessedness
In riches, wealth, and righteousness forever.
Just man, for you comes light to fill your eyes.
Kind man, the dawn will always come and sever
Light from darkness. Each day, the sun will rise.
Mercy, fair dealing, justice, equity,
Munificence—these earn prosperity.

Never will the righteous man be rattled
Or lose his honored name, his reputation,
Persistently faithful when embattled,
Quiet, serene in every situation,
Remaining steady, trusting in the Lord
So fully that he need not fear the worst,
Too safe in God to fear a heathen horde.
(Under God's shield, His people will be first.)
Very generous his gifts to impart,
With kindness for the poor, and without fear,
Xenophobia is far from his heart.
Yes, he is victor, honored. God is near.
Zooming in on this, his foes are whining,
Zero the result of all their pining.

Psalm 113
Magnificat

Sing, "Hallelujah!" Praise Him. Praise His Name.
His servants, praise again. Yes, praise Him yet.
All people, for all time, must know His fame.
From early dawn until the sun is set,
His Name be praised each moment of the day
Above all nations, high beyond the sky.
For who is like our Lord, high, far away,
Who condescends to keep us in His eye,
To see this earth where tiny creatures creep,
And lift that poor man, all forlorn, alone,
Up from the dust, up from the garbage heap,
High up with princes, high upon a throne.
That woman who once had a fruitless womb
Will praise the Lord, her youngsters in the room.

Psalm 114
Tremble, O Earth

His people left Egypt, land of strange speech.
Then did Judah become His holy place,
With Israel inside His dominion's reach.
In panic fled the sea before His face.
Before Him shrank away the Jordan River,
And mighty mountains seemed to skip like rams—
Thus did His power make them shake and shiver—
As little hills were made to leap like lambs.
So why then did you run away, O sea?
And mountains, what could make you skip like rams,
Or river, turn and shrink away and flee,
Or little hills, jump up and down like lambs?
Before the Lord then tremble, earth and mountain.
He makes hard rock become a flowing fountain.

Psalm 115
All Glory to Your Name

All glory, Lord, to Your Name, not to us,
Oh, You Who are forever kind and true.
"Where is their God? We can't see Him!" they fuss.
In heaven, God does what He wants to do,
Unlike a helpless manmade effigy
Of silver formed, perhaps of precious gold,
Appearing good, with eyes that do not see,
With ears that hear not, hands that cannot hold.
Their mouths are mute, their sculpted noses numb.
They have two feet, but they will never walk.
Their makers will be like them, voices dumb,
Dry, lifeless throats incapable of talk.
So trust Him, Jacob's, Aaron's progeny—
Revere your Helper, your Security.

Our Lord knows us, and blessings will accord—
Yes, He will bless the House of Israel
And House of Aaron, all who fear the Lord,
These humble and those mighty ones as well.
Our Lord now make your health and wealth increase,
For you and for the ones you bring to birth.
Receive from Him His blessings and His peace,
Great Maker of the heavens and the earth.
Those heavens He retained to be His home,
But earth below to men and women gave.
No praise will come from those beneath the loam,
Now lying mute and lifeless in the grave.
By us the living He will be adored
Both now and always. We sing, "Praise the Lord!"

Psalm 116
I Love the Lord

I love the Lord. He heard my plaintive cry.
In mercy He has listened tenderly.
Because He paid attention, I know I
Will call on Him while life is left in me.
Afraid of death, in sorrow and in pain,
I cried out loud, entangled in my fears,
Exclaiming, "Save me, Lord!"—and not in vain.
Our Lord has taken notice of my tears.
And when I called on Him in my distress,
He showed to me His mercy and His grace
That worked together with His righteousness
To take away the sadness from my face.
Our Lord did save this simplehearted soul.
When I was brought down low, He made me whole.

Because the Lord is good, my soul finds rest
In Him Who gave me life instead of death.
What I believed I therefore did attest
In my great pain: "Men lie with every breath."
What could I do for God, Who is so good,
But raise the cup and call His Name out loud?
In giving thanks, I gave Him what I could.
I pay the Lord my vows before the crowd.
His people's lives are lovely to His eye.
I am Your slave, my Master and my King
Who freed me from my chains, and therefore I
Will call on You and bring an offering.
I pay the Lord my vows before the crowd
Within the Temple courts. Praise Him aloud!

Psalm 117
Roundelay of Praise

And all you people say with one accord,
"His love for us is great beyond all knowing."
Give God the praise. All people, praise the Lord.
His faithfulness continues, never slowing.
His love for us is great beyond all knowing,
So praise the Lord, all nations everywhere.
His faithfulness continues, never slowing,
And we will dwell forever in His care.
So praise the Lord, all nations everywhere.
Yes, praise Him for His mercy, always sure,
And we will dwell forever in His care,
Believing that His truth will long endure.
And all you people say with one accord,
"Give God the praise." All people, praise the Lord!

Psalm 118
Hosanna

Be grateful to the Lord, for He is good.
His faithful love and kindness last forever.
Let Israel's children tell us, as they should,
"His faithful love and kindness last forever."
As Aaron's priestly sons have understood,
His faithful love and kindness last forever.
Now say, as only those who fear Him could,
"His faithful love and kindness last forever."
I cried out to the Lord to help me here.
In answer, He has kindly set me free.
Since He is with me, I should never fear
What other humans plan to do to me.
My Lord, my Help—beside me constantly—
Now shows me my defeated enemy.

It is wise to take refuge in the Lord,
Yes, wiser than to trust in any man.
It is wise to take refuge in the Lord,
Who shelters as no human ruler can.
All those heathen nations had me surrounded.
I cut them down in the Name of the Lord.
On every single side my way was bounded.
I cut them down in the Name of the Lord.
They buzzed about like bees around the hive.
I cut them down in the Name of the Lord.
Like thorns in crackling flames, they could not thrive.
I trusted God. His help is my reward.
My Lord, my Strength, my Song of jubilation,
Has now become my Savior, my Salvation.

In righteous homes, triumphantly they cry,
"Our Lord's right hand has done amazing things!"
With joy, His prowess is exalted high:
"Our Lord's right hand has done amazing things!"
I will not die. I surely will survive
To celebrate the Lord's great deeds for me.
His discipline is hard. But, still alive,
I see cold death denied its victory.
God opened up the gates of righteousness.
I stand before the Lord's gate, clean and fair.
Soon I will enter in with thankfulness,
For only righteous ones may venture there.
You answered me with mighty liberation.
I thank You for becoming my Salvation.

That stone the builders simply kicked away
Has now become the building's cornerstone.
God's works, for us to see, are on display,
His marvelous achievements clearly shown.
And this is the day that the Lord has made,
A day in which we gladly will rejoice.
Please give us, Lord, the things for which we prayed—
Oh, save us! Let us thrive. Please hear our voice.
May he be blessed who comes in God's own Name.
We bless you from the Temple, as we should.
Prepare the sacrifice, then, for the flame.
Be grateful to the Lord, for He is good.
Yes, I will praise and thank Him, failing never.
His faithful love and kindness last forever.

Psalm 119A
Blessed Are the Undefiled

All happy, those who walk in blameless ways
And from the Lord's true Law do not depart,
Aligning with His witness all their days
And seeking after Him with all their heart.
Avoiding every wrong, they do not sin
As, faithfully, they walk His holy way.
Announcing provisions to hedge us in,
Almighty, You demand that we obey.
Ah, how I wish my ways were always straight,
Always minding all Your prescriptions well,
Ashamed never, if I could truly state,
"All Your commands I keep, Lord, truth to tell."
As I, with praise, Your judgments bring to mind—
And Your prescriptions—leave me not behind.

Psalm 119B
Thy Word Have I Hid in Mine Heart

But how can young men's lives be set apart?
By staying in compliance with Your Word.
Behold, I seek for You with all my heart.
By me let Your commands not go unheard.
Betimes I hide Your sayings in my heart
Because I would not sin against You, Lord.
Blessings and praise to You, Lord—please impart
Beneficent prescriptions to be stored
By heart and mind, so my lips may declare
Before the world the judgments that You voice—
Beyond great riches, far beyond compare.
Believing in Your witness, I rejoice.
Be Your provisions, Your directions heard,
Beloved Your prescriptions and Your Word.

Psalm 119C
A Stranger in the Earth

Cherish me, Your servant, that I may live
Consulting Your Word. In it will I stay.
Close not my eyes, my gracious Lord, but give
Choice insights from Your wondrous Law each day.
Commands from You, so dear, please do not hide,
Considering on earth I am a stranger
Craving judgments from You, my steps to guide.
Cursed are the proud who scornfully court danger,
Commands from You ignoring. Lift from me
Contempt and blame. Your witness is my way.
Chieftains who speak of me insultingly
Count for naught. Your prescriptions I obey.
Counseled am I by Your witness, my Lord,
Cherishing it, and with it in accord.

Psalm 119D
Adhesit Pavimento

Dust chokes off my life and sticks to my soul.
Deliver me, according to Your Word.
Denouncing false ways, I seek Your control.
Disciple me with Your prescriptions, Lord—
Delineate provisions for my learning.
Delight me with Your works. Inspire deep feeling.
Depressed and sad, from every pleasure turning,
Depending on Your Word alone for healing,
Downcast, I beg You, take all lies away,
Delivering Your holy Law to me.
Devoted am I to Your truthful way,
Depending on Your judgments totally.
Desire for Your witness rules out disgrace,
Dear commands that free me to run the race.

Psalm 119E
In the Path of Thy Commandments

Educate me, Lord, in Your righteous way.
Ever Your prescriptions I will observe.
Enable me Your Law to know, obey,
Enthusiastically, heartily serve.
Enjoying Your commands, of them I talk,
Eagerly attempting to do Your will.
Encourage me to witness by my walk—
Erring not, greedy desires to fulfill.
Eyes I turn to You, Lord. Set me apart—
Endless my life, aligning with Your way.
Establish Your sayings. My servant heart
Earnestly reveres You, more every day.
Eliminate shame. Your judgments I love,
Enlivened by provisions from above.

Psalm 119F
According to Thy Word

Fully bestow Your mercies, Lord, on me,
Faithful to Your sayings' promise always,
Flinging back insults flying scornfully
From lips disdainful of Your Word, Your ways.
From me never take away Your Word—*never*—
For in Your judgments all my hopes reside.
Forever I will keep Your Law—*forever*—
Far from breaking it, whatever betide.
Freely I will walk in Your provisions,
Finding liberty in seeking Your will,
Faithful to Your witness—clashing visions
Fearing not—before kings, unashamed still—
For I love, and delight in, Your commands.
For Your prescriptions, I lift grateful hands.

Psalm 119G
Thou Hast Caused Me to Hope

God, think of Your Word to Your servant—me,
Given hope by Your nearness in my strife,
Great comfort in every adversity.
Good Lord, Your sayings have given me life.
Gross mocking from the scornful does not cease.
Governed by Law, I fear no scofflaw bold.
Genuine comfort comes, and so does peace,
God, from Your judgments, as in days of old.
Ghastly to me are wicked mutineers
Going away from the blessings of Law.
Gently, Your prescriptions sang to my ears
Grand truths, whatever far places I saw.
Good night, my Lord. Your Name my only thought,
Guide me by Law, provisions You have taught.

Psalm 119H
I Will Rise to Give Thanks

Here and forever, Lord, You are my all,
Hence I treasure Your Word, within, down deep.
Heartily for Your pardon hear me call.
Have mercy—your sayings' promises keep.
Heavy-hearted due to my unclean hands,
Humbly to Your true witness I return.
Hastily I seek to keep Your commands.
Heathen may mock—Your Law I must not spurn.
How grateful I am! I rise at midnight,
Honoring Your right judgments as I pray.
Happy to have good friends (who seek the right,
Heeding Your provisions), with them I stay.
How vast is Your mercy! It fills the earth.
Help me learn Your prescriptions, know their worth.

Psalm 119I
Thousands of Gold and Silver

In all things You have shown me utter kindness,
In keeping with Your Word, which always stands.
Illuminate me. Take away my blindness.
Increase my faith, my trust in Your commands.
I used to get away with what I could.
In anguish now, Your sayings I digest.
If You are good, then all You do is good.
It's Your prescriptions that are always best.
Is it the arrogant who slander me?
In *my* heart, Your provisions meet with awe.
Implausibly gross their foul hearts must be!
I heartily delight in Your fair Law.
In my deep wounds are Your provisions taught.
In my mind, Your Law like great wealth is sought.

Psalm 119J
Let My Heart Be Sound

Joined all my parts are by Your skillful hands.
Jubilant, I learn Your Word faithfully.
Just give me skill to teach Your good commands—
Joyful will Your people be to see me.
Judgments of Yours are always right, I know.
Justly, out of kindness, You afflict me,
Jehovah, that Your mercy You may show.
Just so do Your sayings, Lord, convict me—
Jolt me—to live in comfort in Your Name.
Jump, does my heart, in delight at Your Law.
Judge the prideful, who are so much to blame.
Justly do Your provisions earn my awe.
Join us who hear Your witness, fear Your Name.
Judge me, by Your prescriptions, without blame.

Psalm 119K
Like a Bottle in the Smoke

Keenly I pine. I wait for Your saving,
Knowing, but for Your sayings, only gloom.
King of Glory, Your Word I am craving,
Kneeling for Your favor and not Your doom.
Kindly deal with me, a dried, leaky bag,
Keeping Your prescriptions, Lord, all the same.
Knowledge, too, I crave: why does justice lag?
Knifelike judgments aim at those casting blame,
Killing my reputation with their lies,
Kicking away Law's righteous, holy bands.
Knock them down—so hateful, with haughty eyes!
Keep me safe, and faithful to Your commands.
Killed were I but for provisions You give.
Keeping Your witness, by mercy I live.

Psalm 119L
Unto All Generations

Lord, by Your Word great Heaven is bounded.
Longstanding is its mighty foundation.
Lasting is the earth that You have founded.
Love flows down to every generation.
Lacking Your judgments, nothing would exist.
Lowly slaves all things are. You are greater.
Lord, without Your Law, what would I have missed?
Life and health and all things, my Creator.
Lord, I cherish provisions that gave me
Light, so that I would not perish sadly.
Look on me. I belong to You. Save me.
Long have I sought Your provisions gladly.
Let Your witness keep me from wicked hands,
Limitless the goodness of Your commands.

Psalm 119M
More Than My Teachers

Meditating on Your Law is my joy,
Minding its wisdom, Lord, all the day long.
My enemies always seek to annoy.
Make me wise. Let Your commands make me strong.
More insight have I than my professors,
Musing long on Your witness as I do,
Much more even than my predecessors,
Morally taught by provisions from You.
My feet are kept from every evil way,
Mighty Lord, as Your holy Word I keep.
May Your judgments not allow me to stray,
Marvelously led by wisdom so deep.
My mouth loves Your sayings, so honey-sweet—
Most wise provisions, not words of the street.

Psalm 119N
A Lamp unto My Feet

Now and always, Your Word will light my way—
Night cannot prevail against its brightness,
Nor can anything. I vow not to stray,
Not at all, from Your judgments' deep rightness.
Needing new life, in Your Word did I trust,
No more in dread of eternal destruction.
Noble Lord, receive my praise. You are just,
Noting that I need judgments and instruction.
Nets have been cast for my life by my foes,
Nasty, foul. Your Law I do not forget.
Near to harsh dangers I am, I suppose—
Never have Your provisions failed me yet.
Next to my heart is Your witness sublime.
Needful are Your prescriptions for all time.

Psalm 119O
My Hiding Place

Odious to me is ungodly thinking.
Obeying Your Law, God, is dear to me.
Outpost, Refuge, Shield—when I am sinking
Out of all hope, Your Word sings lovingly.
(Off with you now, scofflaws, for I will keep
Our God's commands!) Your sayings uphold me,
O God. My heart is unashamed, down deep,
Of Your prescriptions, for You have told me:
On them depends my soul's security.
Over tricksters You trample, to their loss.
Once Your prescriptions purge impurity,
Ore of justice gleams—free of earthly dross.
Oh, Lord, to me Your witness is most dear.
Only You, and Your judgments, do I fear.

Psalm 119P
According unto Thy Mercy

Performing just judgments, I plead, my Lord,
Please do not abandon me. Dear God, please
Protect me, Your servant, with Your sharp sword.
Proud enemies would bring me to my knees.
Pining for salvation, my eyes are wet,
Pleading for righteous sayings. Lord, forgive—
Place me in the heart of Your mercy. Let
Prescriptions of Yours teach me how to live.
Put wisdom in me. Make me understand
Pure words of witness, Lord, that You have spoken.
Past time it is for You to take a hand.
People do not fear You. Your Law is broken.
Provisions from You are priceless, I hold—
Preferred are Your commands above fine gold.

Psalm 119Q
Understanding unto the Simple

Quite wondrous is Your witness, Lord of might,
Quotations memorized that make me whole.
Quietly entering, Your Word brings light,
Quelling ignorance in this simple soul.
Querulously I cried for Your commands,
Quite breathless as I whimpered, without shame,
Quivering, Lord, for mercy at Your hands.
Quit from fear of judgments, I love Your Name.
Quicken by Your sayings my daily walk—
Quash sin's oppression fully, from the start.
Quite safe am I from spiteful deeds and talk,
Quaking not, Your prescriptions in my heart.
Quick, shine Your glad provisions on my head!
Quench tears that for Your broken Law were shed.

Psalm 119R
My Zeal Hath Consumed Me

Righteous are You, Lord, and Your judgments, too.
Righteous is the witness You have given,
Right trustworthy the truth that comes from You.
Rightly do I rage, for I am driven
Raving mad when I see Your Word ignored.
Resplendent are Your sayings—holy, pure.
Recognizing this, I love them, my Lord.
Reputedly, I am base and obscure.
Regardless, Your provisions I observe.
Righteous Lord God, Your Law is always right.
Repressed and troubled—pained in every nerve—
Rallied by Your commands, still I delight.
Righteous, my Lord, is Your eternal witness.
Revive my mind, and let me not be witless.

Psalm 119S
Thou Art Near, O Lord

So broken was I that I cried aloud:
"Stay, Lord, for Your prescriptions I embrace.
Save me!" I cried again, and then I vowed,
"Surely, in Your witness will I find grace."
Still sooner than the sun did I arise,
Shouting, "Lord, in Your Word is all my trust!"
Still late at night I sat with open eyes
So I could study Your sayings, so just.
Sweetly, Lord, hear me in Your loving grace.
Sustaining life Your mighty judgments are.
(Sneaking near now are those who seek disgrace.
So far, Lord, from Your Law they are—so far.)
Soft and near, Your commands speak truthfully,
Strong witness lasting through eternity.

Psalm 119T
According to Thy Lovingkindness

Take pity on my pain, my Lord, and save me,
This one who never would Your Law forsake.
Take up my cause. Acquit me. Lord, You gave me
True life. Your sayings' offer I did take,
Though the wicked Your prescriptions will spurn.
Tender and gracious, Your judgments give life.
Too many hate-filled faces toward me turn—
They cannot dim Your witness in this strife.
Transgressors grieve me, for they have no fear,
Taking Your sayings as nothing but jest.
To me, though, Your provisions are most dear.
Then give me, loving Lord, life at its best!
True is Your Word since eternity past.
Till past the end of time Your judgments last.

Psalm 119U
They Which Love Thy Law

Unjustly have I felt the lash of power.
Under Your Word I freely bend my knee.
Unceasingly, Your sayings, every hour,
Unfailing stores of joy will be to me.
Untruth repels me, O my holy God.
Ultimate truth, Your Law, fills me with love.
Uncounted times, Lord, I will give You laud,
Urged by Your righteous judgments from above.
Undimmed, eternal hope inspires our awe.
Untouched by unbelievers' wicked hands,
Untroubled are the ones who love Your Law,
Urgently pursuing Your good commands.
Utterly Your holy witness I love,
Under Your wise provisions from above.

Psalm 119V
Let My Soul Live

Vouchsafe that You will hear my heartfelt cry—
Vanquish ignorance with Your Word, Your sword.
Valuing my pleas in heaven on high,
Vindicate me by Your sayings, my Lord.
Volumes of wisdom, of Your great prescriptions,
Voluntarily I learn at Your hands.
Voicing Your sayings with vivid descriptions,
Very true and righteous are Your commands.
Vehemently I plead, Lord, for Your aid,
Vital provisions to bring me Your light,
Virtually pining for pleasure delayed—
Vibrant joy in Your Law, utmost delight.
Voluble in praise, in Your judgments living,
Vagabond, I beg—Your commands be giving!

Psalm 120
A Song of Degrees

I call upon the Lord in my distress,
And this I know—He hears me when I cry,
For He is famous for His faithfulness.
Please rescue me, my Lord, from lips that lie,
From tongues that put forth nothing but deceit,
That never care if what they say is true.
What will the Lord do, you who lie and cheat?
Deceitful tongues, what will He do to you?
Do you think you can flee Him, simple souls?
Watch out—He is a warrior. His sharp arrow
Will penetrate your heart, and burning coals
Will pierce your bones with pain down to the marrow.
(As though I lived in Meshech, or Kedar,
I yearn for peace, but people speak of war.)

Psalm 121
Whence Cometh My Help

I look up to the hills. I lift my eyes
To find the place where my relief comes from.
My help comes from the Lord, Who made the skies,
Who made the earth—Who made all things, in sum.
He will protect you, will not let you fall.
This Watchman cannot fail or fall asleep,
Nor will He ever look away at all.
His precious flock, this Israel, He will keep.
Yes, even if the sun should shine too bright,
Protecting shade will fall down from His hand.
And He will still be watching through the night—
In sunshine or in moonlight, safe you stand.
Our Lord will watch, so no harm will affect you.
At home, away from home, He will protect you.

Psalm 122
A Song of Degrees of David

I really did rejoice to be invited
Up to that holy house, the Lord's great hall.
Within your gates your people stand united,
Jerusalem, inside your mighty wall.
Jerusalem is strong and well constructed.
See them ascend, the peoples of the Lord,
To praise His Name, as they have been instructed,
Before King David's throne, with one accord.
So pray. Yes, pray for Jerusalem's peace.
Protect, you holy city, those who love you,
And may they prosper. May their good increase
Within your walls, all those now dreaming of you.
Jerusalem, we pray for peace for you.
Our hearts are there. God's Temple stands there, too.

Psalm 123
I Lift Up My Eyes to You

To You, and You alone, I lift my eyes,
Up past the stars, up to Your most high throne.
I look to You, Who live beyond the skies.
I turn to no one else, but You alone.
A slave will look up to his earthly lord,
A serving maid up to her lady's hand.
So do we look to You, God most adored.
In need of mercy, here we humbly stand.
Then please have mercy on us, great Lord God.
We plead for Your compassion, for Your grace,
As through this hostile, mocking world we plod.
For mercy, Lord, we look up to Your face.
Those proud, complacent ones, the "highly born,"
Have given us our fill of heedless scorn.

Psalm 124
If Not for the Lord

"If God our Lord had not been on our side,"
Let the House of Israel now proclaim,
"If God our Lord had not been on our side
When fearsome enemies against us came,
They would have swallowed all of us alive
In their fierce anger, raging like a fire,
Like roaring waters no one could survive
That would have drowned us, swallowed us entire,
Yes, swallowed us entirely, drenched us, drowned us
Where we would never see the light of day."
We bless the Lord. The wicked have not found us
And have not been allowed to take us prey.
Freed, as a bird from the fowler's net flies,
Our Help is the Lord, Who made earth and skies.

Psalm 125
They That Trust in the Lord

Those who trust in the Lord are like that peak,
Mount Zion. They will not be moved—no, never—
For like that mountain is the Lord they seek,
Who always was, is now, will be forever.
Jerusalem, in a mountainous land,
Protected from its foes, will dwell in peace.
And like a wall, the Lord will cup His hand,
Giving protection that will never cease.
For He will not allow the bad to rule—
He is coming to rid the earth of them.
He guards the good from being evil's tool,
As circling mountains guard Jerusalem.
Do good to the good, send the bad to hell,
And, Lord, preserve the peace of Israel!

Psalm 126
Like Them That Dream

When the Lord turned us and sent us streaming
Back to Zion, back from our long exile,
We were amazed. We thought we were dreaming!
Our mouths could only laugh, and sing, and smile.
And even unbelievers spread the story:
"You see? For them the Lord has done great things!"
For us the Lord has done great deeds of glory.
No wonder that everyone shouts and sings
Great songs of freedom, blissful tunes of gladness.
So turn us, Lord, as You would turn a stream,
And make us free and joyful. End our sadness.
(The good news is that this is not a dream!)
He who goes in tears, sowing as he grieves,
Comes back with glad song, holding golden sheaves.

Psalm 127
A Song of Degrees for Solomon

Unless the Lord constructs the house, no good
Is all the builders' work. Unless He keeps
The town, the best policemen never could.
Then what good comes from one who hardly sleeps,
Who wakes up early, stays up late to worry,
And chooses not to rest within God's peace?
Men, love your children. Why be in a hurry?
Praise God, Who makes your family increase
And brings you children as a precious gift.
So treasure them, as gold from heaven's store.
Our children fly through life (for time is swift)
As arrows fly out from a man of war.
Happy is the man who has a full quiver.
His sons will face his foes and never shiver.

Psalm 128
The Vine and the Olive Tree

Happy are all those who revere the Lord,
Who live their lives according to His ways.
Your labor will bring more than room and board,
And happiness will brighten all your days.
Inside your house, your wife, a fruitful vine,
Your sons like strong and healthy olive trees
Around your table, standing straight and fine—
Your blessings will be these, and more than these.
You will prosper. So will Jerusalem.
Long life will be yours. You will see, as well,
Your children's children. Yes, rejoice in them,
And in God's promise—peace for Israel!
Our Lord, from Zion, all your life will bless
With hope, prosperity, and happiness.

Psalm 129
Many a Time

"Many wounds have I received since my youth,"
May faithful Israel now most truly say—
Many wounds have I received since my youth,
But foes have never prospered, to this day.
Their plows have cut deep stripes into my back,
Have sharply dug their furrows, straight and long.
Our righteous Lord repels each new attack—
He cuts the wicked's cords, for He is strong.
Let Zion's foes turn back in great confusion—
Like grass on rooftops, may they never thrive
(Unlike the grain that grows in great profusion,
That fills our storerooms, keeping us alive).
Let them not hear the customary saying:
"May you be blessed. In God's Name we are praying."

Psalm 130
De Profundis

In deep despondency I cry to You,
Lord, out of places painfully profound.
Let my complaint be one You listen to—
Please turn Your ear to my faint pleading sound.
If You should keep a record of all wrongs,
Then ours would be the fate that we have feared—
But, Lord, if anyone to You belongs,
There is forgiveness. Hence, You are revered.
How watchfully I wait. The drapes are drawn,
Yet, hoping in His Word, I wait for Him
More earnestly than watchmen wait for dawn.
Our Lord will brighten what looks dark and dim.
So, Israel, wait in hope. God will shine in
With love and grace, redeeming you from sin.

Psalm 131
As a Weaned Child

Lord, my heart is not proud, nor are my eyes.
Like a weaned child, I am calm to the core.
I have no need to pry into the skies.
Please let me know Your will—no less, no more.
Some things must stay a mystery to me.
Please let me know Your will—no less, no more—
For I have made my soul go quietly.
Like a weaned child, I am calm to the core.
Please let me know Your will—no less, no more—
For I have calmed my wayward, restless soul.
Like a weaned child, I am calm to the core—
A quiet child, its mother in control.
Like a weaned child, I am calm to the core.
Let Israel hope in God forevermore!

Psalm 132
A Coronation Song in Zion

Remember David, Lord—all he endured.
To You he made a vow to have no rest
Until Your dwellingplace had been secured.
Forgoing sleep, he said, would be his test.
We heard it near the town of Bethlehem—
"Come, to His tabernacle let us go."
We heard it in the fields of Jearim—
"To worship Him we go." Yes, be it so!
Arise then, Lord, up to Your dwellingplace—
You, and the ark that represents Your might.
Let us bow down, our Lord, before Your face,
That we may celebrate You day and night.
Lord, clothe Your priests in robes of righteousness,
Your saints rejoicing in Your holiness.

For David's sake, Lord, honor Your anointed.
To David You have made a certain vow—
His throne to his descendants is appointed
Forever, if they keep Your statutes now.
Our Lord has chosen Zion. Hear Him say,
"This is My dwellingplace eternally—
My throne is here until the final day.
This city's poor will know prosperity.
I clothe the priests of Zion with salvation,
And David's strength will bud, a fruitful tree.
My saints will ever sing in jubilation,
And David's lamp will burn unceasingly.
I clothe his enemies in robes of shame,
But on his head the crown shines like a flame!"

Psalm 133
A Song of Ascents of David

Oh, my, how good it is when brothers dwell
In unity together, giving pleasure
As when the precious oil on Aaron fell
All down his head and beard, that costly treasure
Just plunging down his neck, his priestly mane,
And soaking through his robe down to his feet—
Much as Mount Hermon's dew, as thick as rain,
Runs down its sides in rivulets as sweet
As dew that likewise runs down Zion's flanks
And blesses all the little hills around.
So do we owe the good Lord many thanks,
Whose great commands from Zion do resound,
For thence His blessing does our dear Lord send—
Long life, so long that it will never end.

Psalm 134
A Song of Ascents

Oh, my fellow servants of God, bless Him,
Our Lord, Who blesses us in everything.
Standing nightly in His house, confess Him
Who makes His people want to praise and sing.
Behold Him in His sanctuary. Bless Him,
You ministers who serve Him. Praise His Name!
All day and night, you worshipers, confess Him,
Our blessed Lord, Who merits all acclaim.
In gratitude, affectionately bless Him,
You people, with your holy hands upraised.
He is your Lord. Sing boldly and confess Him
Who made the earth and sky. May God be praised!
And out of Zion may He send His blessing
On you who praise the Lord, His Name confessing.

Psalm 135
Out of Zion

Praise the Lord. Hallelujah, praise His Name!
Praise Him, His faithful servants great and small.
Not only in the Temple give acclaim,
But in the courts around His lofty hall,
Praise the Lord. Hallelujah, He is good!
Sing praises to His Name, for that gives pleasure.
Our Lord chose Jacob just because He *would*,
Chose Israel to be His own dear treasure.
I know the Lord, the mighty Lord, is great—
Yes, greater than all heathen "gods" is He.
Whatever He may please, He can create,
In heaven, on the earth, or in the sea.
He makes clouds arise, sends lightning and rain,
Brings wind from His storehouse as men bring grain.

The firstborn sons of Egypt He struck down,
The firstborn of their people, flocks, and herds.
In Egypt, God's great deeds brought Him renown
Despite the Pharaoh's might, his haughty words.
So many other nations He struck down,
And those who had been mighty kings He slew.
Against the Amorites He gained renown—
Kings of Bashan and Canaan He killed, too.
Then on His people God bestowed their land—
On Israel, His blessed, chosen nation.
Your reputation, Lord, will always stand
Forever, throughout every generation.
Our Lord, we know, declares His people pure—
For His compassion, His great love, is sure.

A heathen idol is an effigy
Of silver formed, perhaps of precious gold,
Poor manmade thing with eyes that do not see,
With ears that hear not, mouth that cannot hold
One breath of air, its sculpted features numb.
Though idols might have legs, they never walk.
Their makers will be like them, voices dumb,
Dry, lifeless throats incapable of talk.
So put no trust in them, those useless toys.
Praise God, O Jacob's, Aaron's progeny.
You House of Levi, make a mighty noise
And praise the Lord with heartfelt piety.
From Zion bless the Lord, God most adored,
Most feared. All Jerusalem, bless the Lord!

Psalm 136
The Great Thanksgiving

Oh, give thanks to the Lord, for He is good—
For His mercy will endure forever—
Lord God of gods, Who does what no one could—
For His mercy will endure forever—
To Him Who by His wisdom made the skies—
For His mercy will endure forever—
Who made the dry land from the waters rise—
For His mercy will endure forever—
Who caused creation to be full of light—
For His mercy will endure forever—
The sun by day, the moon and stars by night—
For His mercy will endure forever.
Give thanks to the Lord, forgetting never
That His mercy will endure forever—

Who struck down Egypt in their firstborn sons—
For His mercy will endure forever—
And brought out Israel, His darling ones—
For His mercy will endure forever.
What His strong hand and outstretched arm could do!
For His mercy will endure forever.
He split the Red Sea, parted it in two—
For His mercy will endure forever—
Where Israel safely crossed, but Pharaoh died—
For His mercy will endure forever—
And still He led them, on the other side—
For His mercy will endure forever.
Thank the King-slayer, forgetting never
That His mercy will endure forever.

And many great and famous kings He slew—
For His mercy will endure forever—
Old Og, the king of Bashan, He killed, too—
For His mercy will endure forever.
Sihon the Amorite fell by His hand—
For His mercy will endure forever—
And on His people God bestowed their land—
For His mercy will endure forever.
He saved us from our foes in our great need—
For His mercy will endure forever—
And God, the Lord, does all His creatures feed—
For His mercy will endure forever.
Oh, thank Heaven's God, forgetting never
That His mercy will endure forever!

Psalm 137
By the Rivers of Babylon

By the rivers of Babylon, our tears
Were shed when they commanded us to sing
Glad songs of Zion. After all these years,
How could our hearts be high, our voices ring?
Although it hurts to think of our lost land,
Jerusalem, stay in my heart and mind—
For I would rather lose my strong right hand,
My tongue, than leave my thoughts of home behind.
My harp hangs silent on a willow bough.
When You restore Jerusalem, my Lord,
Then pay back Edom for her gloating now—
Give Babylon at last her true reward.
She killed infants in the sight of their mothers.
May she be served as she has done to others!

Psalm 138
With My Whole Heart

With my whole heart, my God, I give You praise.
Ignoring false "gods," I sing Your acclaim.
To Your truth and mercy my voice I raise,
Revering Your Temple, Your Word, Your Name.
You will have praise from every earthly king
Who hears the words that come from Your own tongue.
(In wonder at His workings will they sing—
May God's great glory evermore be sung!)
High as He is, the Lord regards the lowly,
But from the prideful He is far away.
Then save me from my foes, my Lord most holy—
May Your right hand reach out to me, I pray.
Your mercy, my Lord, will endure forever.
Your handiwork You will abandon never.

Psalm 139
Words of Eternal Life

You search me, Lord, and know each part of me,
Know when I sit down, know each time I stand,
Know unformed thoughts down in the heart of me.
Better than I, myself You understand.
Wherever I walk, whenever I rest,
Whatever I might say before I speak,
You know better than those who know me best,
Your understanding wonderful, unique.
Such knowledge, Lord, is far too high for me.
Where could I run, Lord, where You would not find me?
Is there somewhere Your Spirit would not be,
Someplace where I could leave You far behind me?
Ascending past the skies, I would find You.
Down in deepest depths You are present, too.

If I could fly to see the sun awaking
Or stay where he lies down at end of day,
There, too, Your hand my hand would still be taking
To lead me, Lord, to guide me on my way.
If I should try to hide in darkest night,
Your eyes would penetrate obscurity
So that the darkness might as well be light.
Into my mother's womb Your eyes could see.
You knew me well, Lord, long before my birth,
When I was in my mother being made,
There hidden as if buried in the earth
Till my young life was fit to be displayed.
On all my lifetime's days Your eyes could look,
Recorded in advance within Your book.

Your thoughts of me, my God, are very dear,
Their number past all guessing, it is true,
Uncountable as grains of sand—and here
I am, awake, alive, and still with You.
But surely, God, the wicked You will kill.
May they be far from me. They have no shame—
They speak against You, blaspheming at will
And showing no respect, Lord, for Your Name.
Do I not hate them, Lord, who show You hate,
Despising those who rise against Your might?
Against them all my hate I concentrate.
Your foes are my foes, meriting my spite.
God, seek out every secret sin in me
And show me how to live eternally.

Psalm 140
Helmet of Salvation

Deliver me from men with evil hearts
Who use brutality to get their way,
Whose energy is spent on sinful arts,
Who stir up conflict every single day.
Their tongues are sharp, like that of any snake.
Toxic are their lips. Venom fills their talk.
Lord, save me from these brutal ones who take
The innocent, in traps laid where I walk.
Their net is spread for me, to trip my feet
And lift me up inside their brutal snare.
They know where my steps and their ropes will meet,
And they have laid them there with wicked care.
Dear Lord, You are my God. To You I say,
"Give ear to me, Lord. For Your grace I pray."

My sovereign Lord, my Helmet of salvation,
You shield my head in battle's fiercest heat.
Do not grant the evil man's supplication
Lest his success inflate his proud conceit.
Upon the heads of those who menace me
May mischief fall from their own poisoned speech
And fiery coals rain down unceasingly.
Throw them in slime pits, far from rescue's reach.
Let evil speakers live in evil fame,
Brutality destroy the brutal heart.
Lord, You will save the needy from all shame,
For You will always take the poor man's part.
Your righteous ones will praise Your holy Name
As You give life to people freed from blame.

Psalm 141
An Excellent Oil

I cry to You, Lord. Hurry to me here.
Please let my small voice carry to You there.
Yes, hear me, Lord—let my cry touch Your ear.
May my words rise like incense on the air,
My prayers like perfumed letters, smelling sweet,
My upraised hands a pleasing sacrifice.
Watch over me with vigilance complete
To keep my mouth from praising sin and vice,
My lips a door with locks, closed firm and tight.
Make my heart never turn to what is wrong,
Nor yearn for wicked friends who spurn the right.
Against temptation make me stand up strong.
Their blows not cruelty, but kindness instead,
Righteous reproofs are like oil on my head.

But hear me when I pray against my foes,
That they may suffer what they planned for me.
For they are not immune, as they suppose,
To justice. They will meet calamity,
Their rulers tumble. Their fall is complete,
Fulfilling those sweet words I prophesied.
Their bones are sown, as one sows grains of wheat,
Down in the dirt along the grave's grim side.
No harvest will result from such a seed!
But my eyes stay on You, my Lord, my God.
I trust in You. Never leave me, I plead,
With those whose bones are rotting in the sod.
My snarling foes—Lord, keep me from them all.
In their own crafty snares cause them to fall.

Psalm 142
David's Prayer from the Cave

My voice is a cry that flies to the Lord,
My voice a plea imploring Him for aid.
Before Him my complaint is humbly poured,
My trouble told, my cry for mercy made.
My spirit weakens. Lord, You know the way
Where I can walk, avoiding hidden snares.
I have no home, no safe place I can stay,
No one concerned for me, no one who cares.
But then I cry to You. I realize
You are my Home, my safe and sheltered Place.
I know that You will not ignore my cries
But rescue me from what I fear to face.
Free me from worry, Lord. I praise Your Name,
Your goodness to me will bring great acclaim!

Psalm 143
A Penitential Psalm of David

My Lord, please hear my prayer. Give me Your ear
And answer me in faithful righteousness.
From Your true judgment keep me free and clear,
For none can come to You in sinlessness.
My enemy has trampled down my soul,
Tormented me, put bad thoughts in my head,
And made me dwell in darkness black as coal,
Left lonely like the long-forgotten dead.
Faint is my spirit, desolate my heart,
But I remember how things used to be,
Recalling all Your good works from the start
And treasuring what You have done for me.
I reach for You with my imploring hand.
For You I thirst, a dry and thirsty land.

So hear me quickly, Lord. My spirits fade.
Then do not turn Your face away from me,
Or I will be like those in death's dark shade.
Your mercy in the morning let me see—
I trust in You to show me where to go.
My soul is Yours, protected, at Your side.
You save me, Lord, from every single foe,
And You are my safe Place where I can hide.
You are my God. Teach me to do Your will,
Your Holy Spirit showing me the way.
For Your Name's sake please keep me living still.
From righteousness, Lord, let me never stray.
Destroy my enemies. Have mercy. Save,
In Your compassion, Lord, Your faithful slave.

Psalm 144
Salvation unto Kings

Praise to my Lord, my Strength, my Rock, my Shield—
You train my hands to go to war for You,
You Tower tall Whose enemies must yield.
In Your strength, God, my foes I will subdue.
Why should You care for humans, why for me?
Why think of us, as fleeting as a breath?
Our life is nothing, only vanity,
A shadow cast by our impending death.
Please bend Your heavens down, and step below.
You touch the mountains. They burst into flame.
Your lightning sends the heathen to and fro—
Your arrows make them fear Your mighty Name.
Reach down. Deliver me from foemen's lies,
Whose mouths deceive, whose handshakes do likewise.

Hear my new song, accompanied by strings,
As I make music to You, God, my Lord.
It is You Who give victory to kings
And save Your servant David from the sword.
Deliver me from every foeman's hand,
Whose mouth deceives, whose handshake does likewise.
Our sons, our youth, like healthy trees will stand,
Our daughters, lovely pillars, upward rise.
Then will our crops, our flocks and herds, increase,
Our barns be filled as full as they can be,
All sadness, all distress, forever cease—
No broken walls, no bleak captivity.
Blessed are those, God, of whom this is true,
This people, Lord, whose only God is You.

Psalm 145
David's Psalm of Praise

Always and forever, my God and King,
Blessing Your Name am I, yes, every day
Calling You great. Your lofty praise I sing.
Down the years let all generations say,
Echoing my words, "Praise God's deeds of glory!"—
For Your great majesty we praise and bless.
God, our descendants still will tell Your story,
Hallelujahs sing to Your righteousness.
I know You choose to love, Your wrath reserve,
Just showing mercy to us wayward ones,
Knowing You give what we cannot deserve—
Love without limit to repentant sons.
Mighty are Your acts. Mighty are our praises.
Mighty thanksgiving all creation raises.

Now, mighty Lord, of Your Kingdom we sing,
Open our mouths to tell Your glory, Lord,
Praising Your eternal rule, most high King.
Quite eagerly Your kind deeds we record,
Recalling, Lord, how patiently we waited,
Sure our needs would come from Your open hand.
The Lord our God has all good things created.
Upon Him call, and near You He will stand.
Very surely He guides the godly's feet,
Willing salvation for those who love Him.
X will mark the wicked man's dead-end street.
Yell God's praises! There is none above Him.
Zither, keep humming as your player sings.
Zephyrs are strumming a song on your strings.

Psalm 146
A Hallelujah Psalm

Hallelujah! Praise God, my faithful soul.
Yes, sing His praise forever, every day.
Do not trust princes. They have no control,
For they must die, and with them dies their sway.
Whoever trusts in Jacob's God is blessed—
That faithful Lord Who made the sky and earth,
Who frees the captive, comforts the oppressed,
Makes blind men see, relieves the poor man's dearth.
Our Lord consoles the victims of the proud
And helps the weak, the foreigner, the sick.
He loves the just, lifts those whose heads are bowed,
And turns aside the wicked's every trick.
Dear Zion, God will reign beyond time's end,
So praise the One on Whom all things depend.

Psalm 147
He Calls the Stars by Name

Praise the Lord. Hallelujah, He is good!
Sing praises to our God, for that gives pleasure.
He builds Jerusalem's lost nationhood,
Gives healing, and gives mercy beyond measure.
He counts the stars and calls them each by name.
God's grasp is infinite, His judgment sharp—
He lifts the meek, but sinks the proud in shame.
Then sing. Give thanks. And harper, sound your harp!
God coats the sky with clouds, the earth with rain,
Makes grass grow on the hills in its due course,
He feeds our flocks, feeds birds when they complain.
Is His delight the strength of man or horse?
No, God delights in those who know His worth,
In all who hope in Him upon the earth.

Acclaim the Lord, Jerusalem, and praise
Your God, dear Zion, for He is your Strength.
He barred your gates, your mighty walls did raise.
He blesses those within your borders' length.
Be true to God, Who gives you His true peace,
Who gives the finest wheat to fill your store,
For it is He Who made your wealth increase,
And you have everything to thank Him for.
At God's command the earth is clothed with snow,
While frost and hail come down as cold as death.
He sends His word, and warming breezes blow,
The melted waters flowing at His breath.
His Word came to Israel—no other nation—
So praise the Lord for His illumination.

Psalm 148
All Creation, Praise Him!

Hallelujah! Praise the Lord, highest heights—
All angels, sun and moon and stars in space,
Waters above the sky, and heaven's lights,
Praise Him Who set you in your proper place.
At His word you came to be—praise His Name,
For His decree will never pass away.
And dwellers in earth and sea, do the same—
All lightnings, clouds, and storms beneath His sway,
All mountains and hills, garden trees and wild,
All beasts both wild and tame, with feet or wings,
Young man, young woman, old man, little child,
All princes, earthly rulers, chieftains, kings—
Praise God, high over heaven, earth as well.
Our Lord lifts up His people, Israel.

Psalm 149
Zion, Rejoice!

Hallelujah! A new song now we sing.
Yes, praise the Lord, O holy congregation.
Zion, rejoice in your Maker and King—
Now praise His Name with dancing, cherished nation.
Keep praising Him with harp and little drum,
With melodies sung out in joyous measure.
Our Lord is happy when He hears us come,
For praises from His people give Him pleasure.
God saves the humble. Saints of His, sing praise
As you bring vengeance with His two-edged sword
Upon the heathen in the coming days
And chain their kings and dukes before the Lord.
To see God's justice to the world restored,
This is His people's honor. Praise the Lord!

Psalm 150
Everything That Hath Breath

Praise the Lord! Praise Him in His holy place.
Praise Him—shout hallelujah!—high above.
Praise Him for acts of greatness and of grace.
Praise Him, for He is God. Praise Him with love.
Praise Him with poetry, with songs and chants.
Praise Him with sounding horn, with harp and lute.
Praise Him with tambourine and graceful dance.
Praise Him with brass, with oboe, and with flute.
Praise Him with drums. Add rhythm to your song!
Praise Him, and let all chiming bells be rung.
Praise Him with crashing cymbals, booming gong.
Praise Him with every song that can be sung.
From all that breathe let heartfelt praise be poured.
Yes, praise Him. Hallelujah, praise the Lord!

"Whither shall I go from thy Spirit? or whither shall I flee from thy presence?"

—Psalm 139:7

Afterword

Here is a good spot to cite John Calvin's view of the Psalms, as quoted in *The Complete Idiot's Guide to Jewish History and Culture*: "I may truly name this book the anatomy of all parts of the soul. For no one can feel a movement of the spirit which is not reflected in this mirror. All the sorrows, troubles, fears, doubts, hopes, pains, perplexities, stormy outbreaks by which the souls of men are tossed, are depicted here to the very life."

This volume completes the *Sonnets of David* trilogy. Thanks be to God! Perhaps some future edition will bind the whole series into a single volume.

Conclusions

One aspect of online publishing is that the publisher does little promotion of an author's work, so that the writer without the wherewithal to invest in advertising must rely largely on word of mouth. Reader, my prayer is that these three volumes have blessed you, and that they will bless others as well.

About the Author

Rev. Robert Hellam, a Congregational minister, is the author of this volume and of *Sonnets of David, Book I* and *Sonnets of David 2*. Bob is an associate pastor at Church of the Oaks in Del Rey Oaks, California, where he teaches an adult Sunday School class. Bob also leads a Wednesday-night prayer meeting. He is a teacher at Monterey Bay Christian School in Seaside, California, where he has taught Bible, English, Spanish, speech, and Latin. Bob was born in Carmel, California, and raised in Seaside, where he lives now. While in the U.S. Navy, Bob and his wife, Connie (with their older son, Chuck), lived in Spain. Bob has been a firefighter, janitor, paperboy, dishwasher, busboy, Census taker, registration assistant, newspaper columnist, city commissioner, unsuccessful candidate for City Council, and a claims representative. He retired from the last-named position after twenty-one years with the Social Security Administration. Bob and Connie's sons are both grown. Chuck and his wife, Claire, live in Killeen, Texas (Chuck is serving on active duty in the Regular Army at Fort Hood), with their daughter—Bob and Connie's first grandchild, the beautiful Malia. At this writing, Bob and Connie's second son, Brian, is about to graduate with a degree in English from the University of California at Davis. Bob enjoys hiking, gardening, genealogy, and stamp collecting. He is a member of the Monterey Bay Colony of the Society of Mayflower Descendants, the Nims Family Association, the Plapp Family Association, and the Methodist Philatelic Society. Bob holds a Professional Educator's Certificate (in English, Bible, and Spanish) from the Association of Christian Schools International. He earned his Bachelor of Arts in English, and his California Standard Teaching Credential, at San José State University; and his Master of Divinity at Western Seminary. He has recently become a doctoral candidate at Trinity Theological Seminary.

Appendix

A feature of the first two volumes that many readers found helpful was the appendix containing the psalms that had been paraphrased in each volume as they appear in the Authorized [King James] Version of the Bible. That feature does not appear in this volume due to space considerations, but readers are invited to look at a King James Bible (or any other good translation) on their own.

Some have noticed that a different edition of the King James Version has been referenced in the Bibliography of each of these volumes. That cited in the first volume was the Bible given me for Christmas when I was ten years old by my grandfather Frank Woodhull Hellam, Jr.; that in the second volume was the family Bible brought over by my great-great-great-grandfather Joseph Hillam, an Irish Methodist, when he and his large family emigrated from Inistioge, County Kilkenny, to Toronto, Ontario, in 1848; and that in the present volume is the family Bible that belonged to my great-grandmother Mary Poessnecker Nims, a faithful member of First Baptist Church in Monterey, California.

Bibliography

The Amplified Bible. Grand Rapids: Zondervan Bible Publishers, 1978.

Blech, Rabbi Benjamin. *The Complete Idiot's Guide to Jewish History and Culture.* New York: Alpha Books, 1999.

Bonhoeffer, Dietrich. *Psalms: The Prayer Book of the Bible.* Minneapolis: Augsburg Fortress, Publishers, 1970.

————. *My Soul Finds Rest: Reflections on the Psalms.* Grand Rapids: Zondervan, 2002.

Carmichael, Amy. *Mountain Breezes: The Collected Poems of Amy Carmichael.* Fort Washington: Christian Literature Crusade, 1999.

Fee, Gordon D., and Douglas Stuart. *How to Read the Bible for All Its Worth: A Guide to Understanding the Bible.* Grand Rapids: Zondervan Publishing House, 1993.

Hellam, Robert. *Sonnets of David, Book I: A Poetic Paraphrase of Psalms 1-41.* Lincoln: Writers Club Press, 2000.

————. *Sonnets of David 2: Books II-III: A Poetic Paraphrase of Psalms 42-89.* Lincoln: Writers Club Press, 2001.

The Holy Bible [King James Version]. Philadelphia: A. J. Holman Company, 1914.

Kushner, Lawrence. *The Book of Words: Talking Spiritual Life, Living Spiritual Talk.* Woodstock: Jewish Lights Publishing, 1993.

LaSor, William Sanford, David Allan Hubbard, and Frederic William Bush. *Old Testament Survey: The Message, Form, and Background of the Old Testament.* Grand Rapids: William B. Eerdmans Publishing Company, 1992.

Lewis, C. S. *Reflections on the Psalms.* San Diego: Harcourt Brace Jovanovich, Publishers, 1986.

Lucado, Max. *Traveling Light: Releasing the Burdens You Were Never Intended to Bear.* Dallas: W Publishing Group, 2001.

Merrill, Eugene H. *Kingdom of Priests: A History of Old Testament Israel*. Grand Rapids: Baker Book House, 1994.

Morris, Henry M. *Treasures in the Psalms*. Green Forest: Master Books, 2001.

Nelson, Marilyn. *Carver: A Life in Poems*. Asheville: Front Street, 2001.

Osborne, Grant R. *The Hermeneutical Spiral: A Comprehensive Introduction to Biblical Interpretation*. Downers Grove: InterVarsity Press, 1991.

Oursler, Fulton. *The Greatest Book Ever Written: The Old Testament Story*. New York: Permabooks, 1959.

Peterson, Eugene H. *Leap over a Wall: Earthy Spirituality for Everyday Christians*. San Francisco: HarperSanFrancisco, 1997.

Ryken, Leland. *Words of Delight: A Literary Introduction to the Bible*. Grand Rapids: Baker Book House, 1992.

Seth, Vikram. *The Golden Gate: A Novel in Verse*. New York: Random House, 1986.

Stuart, Douglas. *Old Testament Exegesis: A Primer for Students and Pastors*. Philadelphia: The Westminster Press, 1984.

Tuck, Gary. *The Arguments of the Books of the Old Testament: With Introductions and Outlines*. Los Gatos: Western Seminary, 1993.

Virgillo, Carmelo, Edward H. Friedman, and L. Teresa Valdivieso. *Aproximaciones al estudio de la literatura hispánica*. San Francisco: McGraw-Hill College, 1999.

Wilson, Mary Elizabeth. *Camp* [a collection of poems]. Minneapolis: Self-published, 1991.

Yancey, Philip. *The Bible Jesus Read*. Grand Rapids: Zondervan Publishing House, 1999.

0-595-28412-4

Printed in the United States
1175400003B/217